NETWORK MARKETING SUCCESS, FAILURE, & EVERYTHING IN BETWEEN

4 HOME BASED BUSINESS TIPS TO ACHIEVE THE LIFE OF YOUR DREAMS

Christopher Mitchell

www.ChangeYourLifeOvernight.com

NETWORK MARKETING SUCCESS, FAILURE, & EVERYTHING IN BETWEEN. 4 HOME BASED BUSINESS TIPS TO ACHIEVE THE LIFE OF YOUR DREAMS.

Copyright © 2017 Christopher Mitchell

ISBN-13: 978-1977888174

ISBN-10: 1977888178

All rights reserved. Under International Copyright Law no part of this publication may be reproduced, stored in a retrieval system or transmitted in any form- digital, electronic, mechanical, photocopy, recording or any other form without the prior written permission of the author or publisher.

Printed In The United States Of America.

TABLE OF CONTENTS:

Introduction:	1
Los Angeles:	9
One Fateful Day:	17
Get To Work:	26
Too Much Pride:	33
Eliminate Pride:	41
Born Again:	45
Unexpected Surprise:	51
Falsely Accused:	57
Filled With Hate:	63
Filled With Happiness:	69
Success Tips:	73

The book you're about to read is an inspiring, true life story about the success, failure, and personal growth experiences that Christopher Mitchell has overcome throughout his many years in the Network Marketing industry. Hopefully, you'll learn from his past and not make the same mistakes that he did. This one of a kind story will motivate and inspire you to continue fighting for your goals and dreams no matter what you might have to go through. If you want to speak to Christopher, or perhaps join his team and have him become your personal mentor, feel free to contact him at his website listed here. God bless you!
www.ChangeYourLifeOvernight.com

Introduction:

My name is Christopher Mitchell. I was born on January 9th, 1979 in Houston, Texas. Two years later, my younger brother Andrew was born. My parents were complete opposites. My mom was an angel from Heaven and my dad, well, like I just said, he was the opposite.

When I was three years old, my dad cheated on my mom. My mom then divorced him and became a single mother. She worked as a secretary at Ohio Wesleyan University in the small town of Delaware, Ohio. With a tiny salary, two young boys, food, clothes, a car, insurance, an apartment, as well as other expenses to pay for, as you can probably imagine, my mom struggled financially to say the least.

She worked full time at her job Monday through Friday and after she would put us to sleep at night she would work on other businesses she did on the side for extra money. She made the best cookies in the world, so she would bake cookies for a few hours each night and then take them to her job and sell them to her coworkers. She also took us to other people's houses once or twice a week and we would have to be quiet and listen to business presentations.

What she was involved in was something I knew nothing about back then as a young boy. However, as I grew older, I realized what she was doing was Network Marketing. I remember her selling Avon and Tupperware. My mom was an entrepreneur. How cool is that? She wanted to be financially free. She wanted to be able to take care of me and my brother more than anything else in the world.

She wanted us to have a good lifestyle. She tried as hard as she could to provide for us. Everything she ever did was to benefit me and my brother in some way. My mom was that person that everyone loved and adored. She would have done anything for anyone.

I remember when I was seven years old, I was sitting on the living room floor with my mom sitting behind me on the couch. I looked her in the eyes and said these exact words that I will never forget for as long as I live:

Mom, I'm going to be rich someday and when I am, I'm going to take care of you and you're never going to have to struggle again. She looked at me with tears coming down her face, said she believed me, and then gave me a huge hug. Just two years later, when I was nine years old, my mom suddenly died from cancer (stress). It took everyone by surprise. She was perfectly healthy one day and then out of nowhere, she was gone. She was only thirty-five years old.

After my mom passed away, my dad automatically regained custody of me and my brother. He had remarried after my mom divorced him and his wife had a daughter of her own.

It was a miserable living situation. My dad and his wife fought every single day without exception. My dad would scream every single time he opened his mouth. He was a terrible dad and a terrible husband. My brother and I stayed out of the house as much as we possibly could because we feared our dad more than we feared Satan. My dad was miserable in life and because of it, he was very hateful and abusive.

I was born with a very outspoken attitude and I don't put up with things that I don't deserve. So, when my dad would yell across the house for me to clean up a mess that he made, I would yell back and tell him no. I told him that he was the one who made the mess, so he needs to be the one to clean it up. He would then start yelling at the top of his lungs, pick me up and throw me across the room. He was violently abusive to me every time that I was around him.

When I became a freshman in high school, I joined the wrestling team and started working out. One day, after I arrived home from wrestling practice, my dad was in one of his usual rages. He started yelling at me to clean the house and I simply said no. Like always, he didn't like that, so he came toward me to beat me yet again, but this time something had changed. I snapped. I was sick and tired of being abused all the time. So, I decided to stand up for myself for the first time in my life. I had gained a lot of size and strength from working out and I had reached my breaking point. I defended myself against my dad. Instead of letting him throw me across the room again, this time, I picked him up and threw him across the room. As he fell to the ground, I ran over to him and put him in a wrestling move that completely popped both of his shoulders out of their sockets. His wife at the time called 911 and the ambulance immediately rushed him to the emergency room. He stayed in the hospital for a few days and when he and his wife came home they kicked me out of the house at that very moment.

I was now fifteen years old and homeless. As a freshman in high school, I didn't even have my driver's license yet. I made some phone calls and ended up moving in with a few of my relatives. I moved in with my Grandparents for a while, then I moved in with an Aunt for a while, and then I moved in with an Uncle for a while. I bounced around back and forth between these relatives houses until I became an official adult.

When I turned eighteen years old, I received a government check from my mom's death. That check allowed me to buy my first car and move into my own apartment. I still had five months until I graduated high school, but I was already living on my own. At this point in my life, I became a loner. I didn't hang out with people anymore. I was a health fanatic who ate healthy and worked out every day, while all of my so-called high school friends either drank beer or smoked pot. I wasn't about to become another statistic who gave up on my goals and dreams in life to become a loser. So, I just stayed by myself all the time.

My life consisted of going to school, working out, and going to baseball practice. I went on to graduate high school just like everyone else, despite bouncing around for three years. I received a free college scholarship from Ohio Wesleyan University in honor of my mom. However, I knew that college would never teach me how to become rich, so I told them to keep it. I passed on going to college and moved to Los Angeles instead.

Chapter One:

Los Angeles

I'll never forget the day when I arrived in Los Angeles, California for the first time. It was Friday, July 4th, 1997 at 11:00 in the morning. After driving across the entire country, I only had forty dollars left to my name. I couldn't believe it. How was I going to survive in Los Angeles with only forty dollars? I was getting sad and depressed very quickly. I decided to go to Gold's Gym in Venice Beach to get in a workout. This place was world famous and known as The Mecca Of Bodybuilding. Since the day my brother and I started working out two years earlier, we had always dreamed of working out at this gym.

When I pulled into the parking lot, I was completely awestruck. I had seen this gym a hundred times before in the bodybuilding magazines, but to see it in person was too surreal. I walked inside and the receptionist told me it was twenty-five dollars for a one-day pass. What, I yelled in disbelief? Are you serious? I couldn't believe it. That left me with only fifteen dollars and I hadn't even been in Los Angeles for an hour yet. Where in the heck was I going to sleep? What was I going to eat? I didn't even care at this point. I just wanted to work out. As I walked past the front desk, my jaw dropped to the floor.

It was a who's who of Hollywood. I immediately saw Hulk Hogan, D.B. Sweeney, Charlie Sheen, and huge bodybuilders Jeep Swenson, Curtis Leffler, Craig Titus, Flex Wheeler, Chris Cormier, Gary Strydom, Danny Hester, and Gunter Schlierkamp all working out at the same time.

After I wiped the drool from my mouth, I walked over to the power rack and started stretching. I told myself that I was going to get in a good workout and then I'll worry about where to sleep afterwards. I put my Walkman on, turned up the volume, and began working out. When I got to my final set of deadlifts with four hundred and five pounds on the bar, a man walked up and interrupted me. I had never seen him before. He asked me my name, my age, and where I was from. I told him my name was Christopher, I was eighteen years old, and I just arrived an hour ago from Columbus, Ohio. I told him I was dead broke and I was going to be sleeping in my car my first night in California. He introduced himself to me. I recognized his name as one of the most famous bodybuilding photographers in the world at the time. He said that I had a lot of potential to become a professional bodybuilder and he wanted to introduce me to someone. He told me to follow him.

As I followed him outside the gym, he led me back to a private, executive office. He introduced me to the owner of the gym. The owner told me to hit some poses and he agreed that I had a lot of potential. He found out about my current situation and told me that I could stay at his house. I followed him home, which was about three miles away. My eyes lit up when I saw his house. Correction! My eyes lit up when I saw his mansion. As soon as I walked inside from the garage, I was speechless. He had the biggest and most glamorous home I had ever seen up to that point in my life. It was truly unbelievable.

He had a four car garage, the ceilings were thirty feet high, and the entire back side of his home was nothing but huge glass windows so you could look out at the Pacific Ocean. I was in Heaven. An hour earlier, I was planning on buying myself a happy meal at McDonald's and sleeping in my car, but now I was inside a million dollar mansion overlooking the ocean. He told me to freshen up so we could go out for dinner. He took me to the nicest restaurant I had ever been to in my life. I felt so uncomfortable. Here I was flat broke, surrounded by rich and famous people, and I didn't even know how to properly cut my steak. No one ever taught me how to hold my silverware in a five-star restaurant before.

We went back to his mansion and he gave me one hundred dollars. He told me to get breakfast in the morning at

The Firehouse restaurant. It's a little hole in the wall that a lot of famous celebrities and bodybuilders eat at. When I arrived at the restaurant in the morning, I ordered the famous Bodybuilder's breakfast. It was steak, egg whites, and buckwheat pancakes. It was healthy and delicious. After I finished eating, I walked over to Gold's Gym to get my workout in for the day. It was Saturday morning and the place was packed! My head was on a swivel. Everywhere I looked, I saw celebrities that I grew up watching on television. It was an awesome experience.

After being at his mansion for a week, he sat me down to have a talk with him. He told me that I had a good, marketable look and a lot of potential to become a huge, professional bodybuilder. However, he said the only way I would ever become a professional bodybuilder was if I took anabolic steroids. He told me not to worry about the cost. He said he would buy me all the steroids I would ever need, I could live at his mansion for free, he'll buy me a car, and I could also train at the world's most famous gym for free. The only thing that was required of me was that I had to work out twice a day and get huge. Once I got huge, he would then call a supplement company and get me an endorsement contract.

What he offered me sounded like a dream come true. However, the only thing I could focus on was the word steroids. I didn't even know what steroids were, but by the sound of his voice it made me think they were extremely dangerous. So, I told him his offer sounded amazing, but I didn't want to take steroids. I asked him if he would still give me the offer if I didn't take steroids? He said no because the only way a person could ever become a professional bodybuilder is if they take steroids. He said that all bodybuilders take steroids. I told him I just couldn't do it. I was afraid and cared about my health too much. He said he understood, but unfortunately, could no longer support me. His job was to sponsor up and coming bodybuilders and help them get huge. He said that if I refused to take steroids then he would be wasting his time with me. So, to make a long story short, my time at his mansion was over.

Chapter Two:

One Fateful Day

A year later, as I was coming out of Vons grocery store on Wilshire Boulevard, in Santa Monica one day, I got stopped by a gentleman who asked me if I would donate some money to a charity he worked for. I reached into my wallet and gave him some money. He then started a conversation by asking me the usual questions that strangers ask each other: what's my name, where do I live, what do I do for a living etc?

I told him I was building up a Personal Training business and just started taking acting classes. He said his name was Bob and he always wanted to get into acting. He asked me if I would take him to my acting class with me? For some reason, I said yes.

Bob didn't have a car, so I started picking him up every week. He and I became good friends. We hung out and went to acting classes together for about a year. Then, as ironic as this sounds, we both ended up moving on the same day and we eventually lost touch with each other. I was broke, but he was even more broke than I was. He was living on someone's couch when I met him and he didn't even have a cell phone. He would call me from the guy's house phone when he wanted to talk to me. So, when we moved, he didn't have a phone to keep in touch with me.

I eventually stopped going to my acting classes out of boredom and just focused on my Personal Training business. I woke up at five o'clock in the morning, went to the gym to train clients all day, and wouldn't get home until nine o'clock at night. That became my life for the next several years. As much as I worked, I still had nothing to show for it. It was now February of 2006. I was twenty-seven years old, still single, living paycheck to paycheck, and extremely unhappy with my life. Sitting in my studio apartment depressed one day, my cell phone rang. It came up as an unknown caller. I've never answered an unknown call before, but my spirit told me to answer the phone. So, I said hello! The voice on the other end asked, is this Christopher Mitchell?

I immediately recognized the voice. It was Bob. Oh my gosh! I couldn't believe it. We were both so shocked, but excited to be reconnected. He asked me a whole bunch of questions to find out what I had been up to the past several years, but as I thought about my answers, I realized my life wasn't any different, or better than when I had last seen him. In my despair, I became silent. In his excited, positive voice, he said, oh Christopher, my life has changed so much you wouldn't believe me if I told you about it. Oh, sure I would. Tell me about it Bob?

Well, I have my own cell phone now. We both laughed. I'm also married and we just had a baby. My wife and I have our own home with a swimming pool in the back yard. At this point, I was in absolute disbelief. I asked him, how in the world have you changed your life so much? He said, well, that's what I want to talk to you about. I want you to come over, see my house, and meet my wife and son. Yeah, absolutely! When? You can come right now if you want? Sure, why not. What's your address? I literally jumped in my car and went to his house that very minute.

When I arrived at his house there was a brand new, sparkling Mercedes Benz in the drive way. I was beyond impressed. He and his successful business partner Leonard greeted me at the front door. They were wearing flashy suits and expensive ties. I was wearing a pair of shorts, a tank top, and a do-rag tied around my head. They told me they were going somewhere and they wanted me to follow them. They got into the Mercedes Benz and I got into my Nissan Sentra.

I followed them to the upscale Doubletree Hotel in Santa Monica. They pulled into the line for valet parking, along with a bunch of other expensive cars. I was in awe! I loved flashy sports cars. I always dreamed of having a Rolls Royce and a Lamborghini ever since I was five years old. Now, they were both right in front of me. I had no idea what was going on at this hotel, but I was excited to find out! Bob and Leonard started introducing me to a bunch of rich looking men in expensive suits. Dressed like a bodybuilder who just finished working out, I felt very out of place. It didn't matter though. Everyone was extremely nice to me. They gave me a name tag and ushered me into a big ball room.

A beautiful woman introduced a man and everyone gave him a standing ovation. It seemed as if he was very wealthy and influential. I was leaning forward in my chair trying to grasp every word that came out of his mouth. He was talking about getting rich with residual income. I had never heard of residual income before. He had me glued to my seat. He said we could get rich from The Deregulation of Public Utilities. He asked the crowd if anyone would like to get paid every single month when people around the world pay their bills? Every hand in the room went up. After the event was over, Bob and Leonard asked me if I wanted to get rich with them?

Well duh, of course I wanted to get rich. I've been dreaming of getting rich my entire life. They said ok, let's get you started. I told them that I didn't have five hundred dollars. They told me if I was truly serious about getting rich, then I would be able to come up with five hundred dollars in an hour. They motivated me with that statement, so I did. I met them at the Starbucks coffee shop on Lankershim Boulevard in North Hollywood, and that's where my Network Marketing career began with ACN. It's a very special day that I will never forget.

They promised me that they would teach me how to get rich in ACN. We would get rich together. Leonard told me that if I just do everything he teaches me to do, millions of dollars will be mine in the very near future. That's exactly what I wanted to hear. I was sold.

Leonard told me there was an international training event coming up in Dallas, Texas in three days and I absolutely had to go to it if I wanted to become wealthy. I told him there was no way in the world I could go to that. I just borrowed the five hundred dollars to start my ACN business and for me to go to Dallas would cost me several hundred more. He told me he didn't have time to waste with tire kickers. So, if I wanted him to invest his time training me, then going to Dallas was non-negotiable. I never had anyone in my life tell me I could get rich before, let alone be willing to help me achieve it, so even though I didn't have a penny to my name, I told him I would be in Dallas, Texas. I ended up jumping on a passenger van at the last second with fifteen other people. One person on the van was a Satan worshipper, while everyone else worshipped Jesus. It turned out to be one crazy drive to Texas.

Once we arrived in Dallas, I ended up sleeping on the floor of a roach motel room for three days. It was absolutely disgusting. I ate nothing but saltine crackers the entire weekend. It should have been a terrible trip, but I was so excited about getting rich that I didn't care about the suffering I went through. I learned the most valuable information of my life from multi-millionaires at that event. It was an inspiring event that I will never forget for the rest of my life.

Chapter Three:

Get To Work

When I arrived back in Los Angeles, it was time for me to get to work. I was determined to get rich fast. I started studying all the top money earners in ACN. I started reading self-help books and listening to personal growth cd's for the first time in my life. I started going to business events several times a week. Whatever my wealthy mentors told me to do, I did. They were rich, I wasn't. They wore expensive, pin-stripe suits, I didn't. They drove flashy sports cars, I didn't. They lived in mansions, I didn't. I wanted the lifestyle that they had. My common sense told me that if I would be willing to do the same things they do, I would eventually have the same things they have.

They told me to do a private business reception in my house, which for me was my studio apartment. I did as they told me to. I invited eight people to my apartment within twenty-four hours of returning from Dallas. Five of the eight showed up. One of my mentors came over to my apartment and did the ACN business presentation for me. He did this because he was successful and I was brand new. My only job was to edify him to my contacts and let him do all of the explaining. It's an amazing partnership. My mentor not only wanted me to get rich, but he personally helped me every step of the way. He didn't succeed unless he helped me succeed. All I had to do was be 100% coachable. Just do what he told me to do and then cash the paychecks that come in. I fell in love with ACN from day one.

Of the five people who showed up, two of them invested $499 and started their own ACN business with me, while the other three supported my business by giving me their bills to enroll on my ACN online storefront. They helped me get promoted and I helped them save money on all the essential services they have to pay for every month.

I got promoted to the position of Executive Team Trainer in my first six days of being in ACN. By doing that, I earned a $1,000 bonus. I then went on to get promoted to the position of Executive Team Leader in my first thirty days of being in ACN, which resulted in earning a total of $4,000. That's absolutely amazing! Most people who graduate college with a degree don't earn $4,000 a month working full time, but here I did it in ACN on a very part time basis.

Watching and studying my mentors my first month in ACN allowed me to learn what to say and how to say it. I simply copied everything they did. I was a great baseball player in high school. However, in order for me to play ball, I had to keep my grades up. Otherwise, I would be ineligible. So, I found someone smart and just copied off him all year long. About a month before the year was over, I got caught cheating. The principal suspended me from school for three days. I mean, are you serious? They punished me for wanting to copy someone who got better grades than I did. That's how screwed up the world is. However, when I started copying my mentors in my business, ACN rewarded me by sending me paychecks. That's the way it should be in life. Network Marketing is how the world should operate.

I absolutely love ACN. I mean, who wouldn't? Everyone in the world pays for TV, Gas, Electricity, Cell Phone, High Speed Internet, and a Home Security System. Being an ACN independent business owner pays me residual income every single month when people all over the world pay their bills. It's a truly recession proof business. No matter what's going on in the economy, people will never stop using these services. That's guaranteed income for people who own an ACN business.

I committed myself to my ACN business as much as I committed myself to anything else in my lifetime. By the end of my first year in ACN, I had hundreds of business partners around The United States and I was getting paid on over one thousand customer's bills every month. I recruited someone onto my team in Chicago and since I was so young, naïve, and hungry, I simply picked up and moved there at the drop of a dime. I had just bought myself a new car and now I was driving it across the country in the middle of winter. I arrived in Chicago feeling so confident. I knew I was about to get filthy rich taking over the windy city. A week after I arrived, I was driving to Ohio for a business event. While passing through the state of Indiana on I-80, my tires went over some black ice. My car went air borne and started spinning out of control. My passenger and I woke up to the sounds of loud sirens and the jaws of life cutting my car to pieces. There was shattered glass from the windshield embedded throughout my entire body. I was on top of the world one minute, and the next minute I'm in an ambulance.

In a split second, my life had changed for the worse. Depression set in very quickly. After we got out of the hospital, I ended up moving into an old, beat up trailer with someone I barely knew. It was pure hell. It was in the middle of the ghetto in the worst part of Chicago. I literally disappeared from life. No one in the world knew where I was. I didn't respond to anyone's phone calls or text messages. A year later, my ACN business had completely diminished.

Chapter Four:

Too Much Pride

I lived in complete depression for an entire year after my car crash. Most of the time, I didn't even leave the trailer I was living in. I had hit rock bottom financially. I didn't even have a dime to my name and on some days I didn't have a single meal to eat.

Finally, I think out of desperation, I told myself that I had to start doing something with my life again, but I had no idea what. I refused to work at a job because I was absolutely, forever unemployable. Too much pride kept me from going back to ACN. I just couldn't get myself to apologize to my friends and mentors in the company after I ignored their texts and phone calls for an entire year because of my depression.

ACN taught me how amazing life was with residual income, so I set out to join another Network Marketing company. Ironically, what I think about, I bring about. So, while walking through a coffee shop one day, I noticed a man giving a business presentation to another man at one of the tables. I knew it had to be Network Marketing. So, I walked right up to the guy and simply told him, I want to join your company. Will you mentor me? You should have seen the shock on his face.

Here he was doing a presentation for someone, trying to convince him to join his company, and out of nowhere he has me walk up to him and say, sign me up. It had to be a dream come true for him. The product he was selling was Tahitian Noni Juice. So, that became my second Network Marketing company. Like most companies in the Network Marketing industry, Tahitian Noni Juice was a good product. However, I had to adjust from marketing essential services that everyone in the world was already using when I was in ACN, to convincing people to try some exotic fruit juice from Tahiti that they've never heard of before. It wasn't easy. My mentors in ACN had groomed me to be a leader. The gentleman I signed up under in Tahitian Noni International wasn't quite on my level when it came to Network Marketing. So, I had to seek out the top money earner in the company and go straight to him. He was a multi-millionaire who lived in a mansion in Atlanta, Georgia. He drove flashy sports cars and painted massive vision. He was my type of guy. At the company's annual convention, I walked straight up to him and said, I'm only going to stay in the company if you agree to become my personal mentor. He must have felt my seriousness because he agreed. I was probably the only dead broke and close to homeless person he ever mentored. I committed myself to my Tahitian Noni business, but it just wasn't the same as ACN. I wasn't as passionate or excited about Tahitian Noni Juice the way I was with ACN.

I was getting ready to leave Tahitian Noni and look for another company when my mentor told me to join in on an emergency team conference call. He dropped the bomb on everyone that he was leaving Tahitian Noni and going to a company called Monavie. He said that Monavie was going to be way better for us as a team. So, all of his top leaders and I left Tahitian Noni and followed him to Monavie. For the next twelve months, I started drinking Monavie and tried to build another exotic fruit juice business. My feelings of discontentment remained. I just wasn't passionate or excited about fruit juice. I then received a phone call one day from my mentor's personal secretary. She said my mentor had some exciting news he wanted to share with me, but he wanted me to meet him in Dallas. She said my flight, hotel, and all my food would be paid for. Wow! Now I was excited.

A few days later, I was on a flight to Dallas, Texas, but I had no idea for what. A limousine picked me up at the airport and took me to an unbelievable mansion. I met up with my mentor and all of his other top leaders, and he introduced us to a billionaire named Trey White. Trey had just invested some of his money and started a brand new Network Marketing company selling some healthy, enzyme filled bottled water called Evolv. He wined and dined us like we were celebrities. Of course, I enjoyed it and the bribe worked for getting me to leave Monavie and follow my mentor into Evolv.

Evolv was now my third Network Marketing company in the last fifteen months. My friends and family were not very supportive of me when I asked them to buy a case of bottled water that cost a hundred and fifty bucks. Evolv was expensive and after a few months with the company, I regretted the decision. Not long after I joined Evolv, my mentor had a team conference call telling us he was now leaving Evolv and going to another Network Marketing company.

This went on for several years. Every time I left a company and then joined another one, I lost credibility with my friends and family members. I started to resent my mentor because I was simply following him as my upline leader and not even thinking about what I was doing. However, it was time for me to take responsibility and grow up. I had to start making my own decisions and stop following others and become a true leader.

So, five years after my car crash, ten Network Marketing companies later, and a lot of unfulfillment, I decided to put my pride behind me and humble myself. I was sick of bouncing around from company to company trying to convince people to buy the latest and greatest lotion, potion, diet pill, or pair of bullet proof pantyhose. I hated product based companies. They just didn't make sense to me.

I didn't know anyone in the world who drank Noni juice, enzyme rich bottled water, put fat wraps around their bodies, or swallowed a pill that makes your stomach expand so you stop eating to lose weight. However, I knew that billions of people watch tv, use gas and electric in their homes, browse the internet, talk and text on a cell phone every single day, and swipe a debit or credit card to buy things with. ACN wasn't just business sense, it was downright common sense. People use these services every single day of their lives, they have to pay these bills every single month for the rest of their lives, and I can get paid every month these bills get paid. Uh duh, that's a no brainer! It was time for me to go back to ACN.

Chapter Five:

Eliminate Pride

In the Holy Bible it says that: Pride goes before destruction, a haughty spirit before a fall. Proverbs 16:18

In the dictionary it says that: Pride is the state or feeling of being proud.

Both of these are correct when it comes to describing my actions of why I left ACN after my car crash. My mentors were great people. They were kind, generous, understanding, and as mature and professional as any group of people could be. It was my own pride that kept me from responding to their texts and phone calls when they were trying to find out where I was. It was my own pride that kept me from apologizing to them after I finally dug myself out of the depression I was in. All the wasted time and discontentment I felt from bouncing around from company to company during that five year period was all my fault. Now that I was more mature and willing to humble myself, I absolutely had to apologize to my mentors in ACN and ask them if they would receive me back into the company and onto their team. I missed being around them so much and ACN was the only company I ever loved and truly believed in.

I picked up my phone and dialed Leonard's phone number. Much to my surprise, he answered the phone exactly like this: Mr. Mitchell, how are you brother? It's been a long time. I've been expecting your phone call. You have, I responded? Yes, I have. Are you ready to get back in ACN? Yes, I absolutely am! How in the world did you know? I knew because there's no other company in the world like ACN and I knew it was just a matter of time until you returned. So, welcome back! Thank you so much! I'm so sorry for ignoring you and letting pride keep me down. I've been miserable for the last five years going to so many different companies. Where can I meet you so I can get my ACN business started up again? I met him an hour later and got back in ACN for good. The date was February 26th, 2011.

I was so happy to be back in ACN. I missed everything about it; the founders, my mentors, my friends, the services, the training events, and of course, the compensation plan. My mentors would help me every step of the way, but because of my actions over the previous five years, I had a lot of work to do. When you bounce around from one company to another company as many times as I did, you lose credibility with everyone. I was now an official member of the NFL: No Friends Left. Now, I was simply going to have to increase my skill set and work ethic to make up for what I lost, which was all my friends and family members. It's ok though. I did this to myself and now I take full responsibility for my actions.

When I rejoined ACN for my second and final time on February 26th, 2011, I was in the same financial position that I was in when I started ACN the first time five years earlier: BROKE!

I was now sleeping on someone's couch in Culver City, California. I didn't have any money or credibility, but what I did have was an ambitious desire for success and an attitude of gratitude that I had been given a second chance. I wasn't going to take that for granted ever again.

Chapter Six:

Born Again

Getting a second chance with ACN was like being born again as a Christian. I was forgiven, my past was behind me, and I was brand new all over again. It also meant I had to start from scratch again. Since I no longer had any credibility, I was going to have to start building new relationships. I'm generally shy, quiet, and a loner, so I was going to have to get out of my comfort zone and start approaching people. I didn't look forward to this, but knew I had to do it if I wanted to change my life and become successful in ACN.

The first thing I had to do was to get myself qualified so I could start earning bonuses and residual income in ACN's compensation plan. This is really simple to do, even for someone like myself who had destroyed all his relationships. All I had to do was enroll a few services on my online storefront. I signed up my own cell phone bill, which is all I had in my own name at the time, as well as my dad and brother's tv, gas, electric, and cell phone bills. There, now I was more than qualified. Just like that, I generated my first bonus.

Now it was time to start recruiting new business partners. I didn't get promoted to ETT and ETL as quickly as I did my first time around, but I didn't have a short-term mindset either. So, I just kept putting one foot in front of the other and slowly but surely started building a successful business again.

I started getting myself plugged back into the weekly business events. This helped me mentally and increased my skill set. I spent as much time as I could around my mentors Leonard and Efrain so they could teach me everything I needed to learn. They had almost forty years of Network Marketing experience between the two of them and they were both top money earners in ACN. I was extremely blessed and thankful to have them in my life. If you're in Network Marketing, or plan to get involved in the industry, the number one thing you'll need to be successful is the right mentor. Having a successful mentor teach you what you need to know is absolutely priceless. Unfortunately, most people who join a Network Marketing company never have a successful mentor as their coach. They have their broke friend or cousin as their coach and it's no wonder why they don't succeed. There's nothing wrong with letting a broke friend or family member introduce you to Network Marketing, but you definitely don't want them to be your mentor. It would be like the blind leading the blind. Neither of you know what you're doing. You need someone who's already had success.

As I started making progress and built my business back up to where it once was years earlier, I decided to leave California and move to Florida. I had lived in California for the last fourteen years and was ready for a different environment. I loved being near the ocean, so Florida is where I decided to go. I chose the Palm Beach area. It's extremely wealthy just like Los Angeles, but much slower paced. At this point in my ACN career, I had created a system for recruiting people that was getting attention from my mentors. I turned my weakness into a strength and I was becoming one of the top recruiters in ACN. As soon as I arrived in Florida, I started building a team. I was now recruiting so many new business partners that I had to start putting them underneath my other business partners. This benefitted not only myself, but other people on my team who weren't quite as accomplished at recruiting like I was. Imagine you wake up one day and realize your mentor (me) had sponsored some new business partners and put them underneath your position. You not only get credit for it, but paid for it. That's called FREE money. Wouldn't that motivate you to stay in Network Marketing? You better believe it would. My successful mentor Efrain did this for me during a time when I was about to quit and now because of it, I have a huge team in Mexico. He was very strategic in doing this. He knew I would never quit if I was constantly getting paychecks. Guess what? He was right.

Since I had increased my skill set, I was now doing for others what Efrain had done for me. It's a way of paying Efrain back. You reap what you sow. Efrain had sowed into my life when I was at rock bottom and now I was able to sow into others. The Law Of Sowing And Reaping is a universal law that will not return to you empty. If you do good to others, you will most definitely have good come back to you. Adopt this principle and live by it. It will change your life forever.

Chapter Seven:

Unexpected Surprise

While living as a bachelor in Florida, minding my own business and enjoying my life, I unexpectedly received an email on Facebook one day from a female friend of mine that I grew up with in Ohio. I hadn't talked to her in over fifteen years. She saw that I was living down in Palm Beach and wanted to come visit me. She and her girlfriend Stacy bought a plane ticket and came down to see me. Throughout the week that they stayed with me, I caught up with my childhood friend and learned a little bit about Stacy too. Stacy was a Registered Nurse at Ohio State University Medical Center. She was recently divorced and a single mother of a little girl. She hated her life in Ohio. She was sad and depressed from what she had gone through in the last couple of years. She had over fifty thousand dollars of debt and couldn't see a way out. However, I was completely debt free and living the good life. She wanted the life that I had. She wanted to be able to retire from nursing so that she could be a stay at home mom for her daughter.

Throughout our conversations, she learned that I had a home-based business with ACN and that I earned residual income. She told me that she had always wanted to earn residual income with a home-based business of her own and wanted to know if I would come to Ohio and help her? I told her no. I loved Palm Beach and didn't want to leave to go to Ohio. Their vacation ended and I drove them to the airport. A week after they flew home, the Holy Spirit spoke to me in a dream to go to Ohio immediately and help Stacy build a successful ACN business of her own. I was obedient. On Friday, August 2nd, 2013, I flew to Columbus, Ohio to start expanding my business there with Stacy being my first business partner.

I mentored Stacy on a part time basis around her full-time job as a nurse. She would work a twelve-hour shift at the hospital and then have me do ACN presentations for her friends, coworkers, and family members after work and on her days off. She kept me busy. Her job was to edify me and my job was to enroll new business partners for her who wanted more time, money, and freedom in their lives. I was spending a lot of my time with Stacy teaching her the business. She and I became very close and her ACN business was growing every day.

My personal business was thriving in Ohio, so I decided to stay for a few more months. After being in Ohio for four months, the Holy Spirit spoke to me in another dream. This time, God told me the reason he had me come to Ohio was so I could meet my wife. He said Stacy and I were going to become husband and wife. I woke up in the middle of the night and said to myself, what a weird dream. Stacy wasn't even my type.

However, the very next night, I had the same exact dream again. The night after that, I had the same exact dream again. I ended up having the same exact dream for three weeks straight. I finally told Stacy that I needed to talk to her. She and I met in person and she asked me what I needed to talk to her about? I said, well, you're not going to believe this, but, I've been having the same exact dream for the last three weeks straight. She said, ok why are you telling me? I said, I'm telling you because the dream is about you. She asked me what my dream was about? I told her that God said she and I were going to get married and become husband and wife. Her mouth fell wide open.

Oh my gosh she responded. I don't know what to say. I'm speechless. I don't know how I feel about this. I need some time to process this. I said, take all the time you need. You're not even my type Stacy. I just wanted to tell you because I don't want to have this dream anymore. A few days later, I was at Stacy's apartment talking to her about business and she interrupted me. She said, I want you to kiss me so I can see how I feel. What? I yelled in disbelief. Kiss you! Are you crazy? If I kiss you then you will want to marry me. Ok, prove it. Kiss me, she said. Fine. Come here. As she came closer, I paused and asked her, are you sure you want to do this? If I kiss you it's going to change everything between us. I know. I want that she said. Ok, you asked for it. We then inched ourselves closer until our lips locked together. We kissed for the next two hours straight. From that moment on we became inseparable.

A year after I arrived in Ohio, on August 28th, 2014, Stacy and I got married. She retired from nursing and we started building our ACN business together full time. Our business grew all over the country. We started traveling and expanding our business in Detroit, Chicago, Cincinnati, Pittsburgh, and New York City. Life couldn't get any better for us, but boy oh boy was it about to get worse.

Chapter Eight:

Falsely Accused

What a difference a year can make. We were living on top of the world in 2015, only to have it all taken away from us in 2016. My wife and I live our lives for Jesus Christ. However, the god of this world is Satan. So, when we started prospering for The Kingdom Of God, we became an immediate target for the devil. The more money we make, the more damage we do to Satan's kingdom. To get back at us for the damage we caused him, Satan decided to use one of his followers to destroy us.

On Monday, April 18th, 2016, we had an unexpected visit at our home by two Columbus police officers. They had an emergency court order in their hands to physically take Stacy's daughter Reese away from us immediately. Not one of us knew what was going on. The police had no explanation. They said they just had to obey orders. Reese was kicking and screaming at the top of her lungs, begging the police officers not to take her away from us. The two police officers felt so terrible for Reese that they called their sergeant and begged him to not have to take her away, but he said they had to. Reese was bawling her eyes out, Stacy was losing her mind, and I was getting ready for war.

We didn't know anything until two weeks later when we were scheduled to appear in court. At our hearing, Stacy's ex-husband stepped up to the witness stand and told every lie he could about me, while he was under oath. He said Stacy and I were porn stars and we were allowing Reese to be a part of this at our house. He said I was a child rapist. He said I was a professional scam artist. He said I was taking massive doses of anabolic steroids, which caused me to be extremely violent and a dangerous threat to society. He said I didn't even possess a driver's license, let alone own a car.

Every single word he said was a lie from the pit of hell. Stacy then explained on the witness stand that every single word he said about me was actually the truth about himself. She said, I was married to him for twelve years. I know him better than anyone. He tried to get me to watch pornography and take me to swingers parties with him all the time. My husband Christopher has never done anything like that. When our attorney asked him where all his evidence was, his counsel objected. The magistrate completely ignored our attorney. Without any evidence against us whatsoever, the magistrate ruled on Stacy's ex-husband's behalf and treated us like we were cold blooded killers. I was now labeled as a porn star, child rapist, and a dangerous threat to society. I was not allowed to be anywhere near Reese per court order. Stacy and I had been betrayed beyond our wildest imaginations. We had our legal rights stripped from us. Stacy's daughter would not be coming home.

Not only did we get falsely accused in a court of law, have Stacy's daughter taken from our home with brute force, but all of our ACN business partners immediately quit our team as well. Nothing was making sense at all. Our business partners loved us and respected us greatly. We were not only their mentors, but their close friends as well. For our team members to quit on their goals and dreams for no reason was producing nothing but a big red flag. Our ACN business began to crumble and we lost everything. Our residual income vanished. We had to sell both of our Lexus' to meet the demand of all the court costs and attorney bills. We could no longer pay our mortgage, so we lost our home as well. It wasn't until a year later and a loss of two hundred thousand dollars that we discovered some terrible evidence.

One of my previous best ACN business partners had called me and Stacy to tell us something. The first thing he said was that he was sorry for believing all the lies and to please forgive him. We didn't know what he was talking about, so we asked him to explain? He said, my ex-wife had conspired with Stacy's ex-husband to destroy you for kicking her off your ACN team a couple of years earlier. I never believed that she would cheat on me, so I believed her instead of you. Unfortunately, not long after that, I ended up catching her cheat on me with several different guys. One day, she just packed up a bag of clothes and left me and her daughter behind. She hasn't returned since.

He went on to say that his ex-wife and Stacy's ex-husband contacted all my other ACN business partners and told them the same lies that were told about me in court; that Stacy and I were porn stars, I was a child rapist, I was a professional scam artist, and that I was extremely violent and a very dangerous threat to society. Not only that, but they decided to slander my name and reputation all over the internet on social media and big, gossip columns as well.

Chapter Nine:

Filled With Hate

Since that unforgettable day back on April 18th, 2016, Reese has been taken away from us, I've been falsely accused in a court of law, I've had all my ACN business partners quit on me, I've had to sell both of our cars, we lost our home, my name and reputation has been slandered all over the internet, I've been thrown into the back of a police car and taken to jail, and my wife and I signed divorce papers to end our marriage. To say that I've been absolutely filled with hate is an understatement.

I've believed in Jesus and proclaimed to be a Christian my entire life. I've always given tithes and offerings to my church, and I've blessed others every opportunity I could. I asked

God, why am I going through all of this? Why and how did this happen to me? Why haven't you done anything? How can the court be so corrupt and not rule in our favor when we have so much evidence to prove that we're completely innocent?

I started to hate God. I started to doubt his existence. I started to hate my wife. I started to blame her and the choices she made in the past for everything I've gone through. I started to hate my life. I started having thoughts of suicide. I started praying that I would die.

I stopped working out. I stopped eating healthy. I stopped having goals. I stopped reading my Bible. I stopped going to church. I stopped wearing my wedding ring. I stopped getting out of bed. I stopped caring about anything. I just wanted to die.

I hated everything. I blamed everything. I gave up on everything. My life started to deteriorate in every area imaginable. I quit my ACN business and gave up on life. I no longer had any friends because I didn't want any friends. My wife actually packed up her things and left me. I had hit rock bottom, again.

I was betrayed, falsely accused, and then became offended. Once I became offended, there was nothing that God could do for me. I had cut off The Kingdom Of God through my offense. It wasn't until my wife had read a book and then bought another copy and had it shipped to me that I learned why my life had spun out of control. This book has changed my life so much that I have to give it a shout out and hope that you will get it for yourself, or someone you know whose life might be out of control.

The book is **THE BAIT OF SATAN** by John Bevere. As soon as I started reading that book, The Holy Spirit convicted me. I had become filled with hate because of everything that had happened to me, then I became offended, and then I refused to forgive my accusers and started playing the blame game. Once I did that, Satan took control of my life.

My wife, who was living with her parents two hours away when she had the book shipped to me, read the book at the same time I did. Both of us simultaneously repented and asked each other for forgiveness. As soon as we forgave each other and everyone else (Stacy's ex-husband, my ex-business partner, the police officers, the magistrate, and the guardian ad litem on the case), we started to prosper in every area of our lives again.

One of my favorite stories in the Holy Bible is that of Joseph. You can read his entire story throughout the book of Genesis. However, let me touch on a few things. Joseph was Jacob's youngest son. Joseph was also a dreamer. His brothers despised him. Instead of killing him, which they wanted to do, they sold him to the Ishmaelites for a profit. He was then sold again to Potiphar. Potiphar's wife then falsely accuses him of trying to rape her and has him thrown into prison. While Joseph is going through this, his father thinks he is dead. Pharaoh eventually put Joseph in charge of the entire country of Egypt. The Holy Bible never said if Joseph got offended by what he was put through, but since he was human, I'm going to assume he did. However, like me, he was constantly having one bad thing happen to him after another, but eventually, Pharaoh put him charge of Egypt. So, I'm guessing if he did get offended he must have released the offense and learned to forgive at some point. Otherwise, he probably would have never had the huge door of opportunity open for him like it did with Pharaoh. Joseph forgave and then he prospered. My wife and I finally forgave and then we started to prosper again.

So, I pray that if you are holding onto any hate, bitterness, resentment, or unforgiveness toward anyone in this entire world, that you forgive them, release them, and actually bless them for what they have done to you. By not forgiving someone for what they've done to you, you're actually only hurting yourself. Not forgiving someone is like drinking poison and expecting the other person to die. Forgive and you will set yourself free.

Chapter Ten:

Filled With Happiness

As soon as I emptied myself of hate, I immediately became filled with happiness. Once I became filled with happiness, everything not only got restored, but God started blessing me more than ever before. My wife returned and we never went through with the divorce. I started making new friends and old friends came back into my life. People all over the world are seeking me out and joining my ACN business. I'm now happier, healthier, and wealthier than I've ever been. Letting go of offense has been the key for everything in my life turning around.

I hope you've enjoyed this short book about my success, failure, and everything I've gone through since I joined the amazing industry of Network Marketing. Becoming successful in Network Marketing was obviously not easy for me as you have now learned. However, it was the road that I had to travel and thankfully, I persevered.

Your road to success in Network Marketing will be different than mine. Maybe it will be easier, I sure hope it's easier, maybe it will be harder, but whatever your road to success is like, don't ever give up. The only way you can fail is if you give up.

If you're brand new to Network Marketing, you've more than likely got involved because of the possibility of earning residual income. I know that's the reason why I got involved. There are very few ways a person can earn residual income. I've been blessed to learn how to receive residual income from two of these ways. One of these ways is through ACN and the other way is by becoming a self-published author. I can teach you how to do both.

If you're not involved with a Network Marketing company right now, or if you're not happy with the Network Marketing company you're involved with right now, please know that you are welcome to reach out to me and join my team. My wife and I would love to have you. We would be more than happy to mentor you personally.

If you have a cell phone, use gas or electricity, watch tv, browse the internet, have anything in your house worth securing, or ever use a debit or credit card as a form of payment, then you're already involved in ACN. Don't you think it's time you start getting paid? If so, contact me!

If you want more time, more money, and a lot more freedom in your life, getting involved with ACN could be the greatest thing you ever do for you and your family. Like most people in the world today, Stacy and I were both overworked and underpaid in our previous careers. We prayed to God that he would send us a way of escape and when he led us to ACN we immediately jumped on the opportunity. I hope you do the same. Stacy and I are not only looking for people who want to make a lot of money, be able to fire their boss, and be able to work from home full time, but people who want to become lifelong friends with us so we can work together and make a difference in this world that we live in. If that's you, watch the video on my website, then pick up the phone and call me.
www.ItsTimeToGetRich.com

Chapter Eleven:

Success Tips

In this final chapter, I would like to give you my personal success tips that I've learned over the years. I know they work from personal experience. If I can keep you from experiencing any of the same setbacks that I've had to endure, then I will be forever happy to have been able to help. Implement these tips into your own Network Marketing business and you will succeed.

1. **Choose the right company**. You must be open minded here and not just assume your company is the best because you're in it. Every Network Marketer thinks their company is the best. However, have you ever been in any other Network Marketing company besides the one you're in

right now? Ok, if you haven't, then you need to remain open minded. You can't possibly say that your company is the best, or it's the right company for you if it's the only company you've ever been a part of. I'm glad I've been involved with ten different Network Marketing companies. It taught me a lot about people, products, training, infrastructure, and compensation plans. For me to start with ACN, go to ten different companies, and then come back to ACN should tell you a lot. I came back for a reason. A lot of reasons! So, make sure you choose the right company. To do this, you must research other companies.

2. **Choose the right mentor**. Having the right mentor is even more important than being with the right company. Your mentor is going to be responsible for a lot of your success

or failure. Poor people can't teach others how to become rich. So, if your poor mom, dad, brother, or cousin introduced you to Network Marketing, that's perfectly fine, but just don't let them be your mentor. If they don't drive the car you want to drive, don't live in the house you want to live in, don't earn the amount of money you want to earn, and haven't become successful in Network Marketing themselves, then they are not going to be able to teach you how to achieve your goals and dreams. Find someone who is already successful, living the lifestyle that you want to live, and ask them to become your mentor. Chances are, they will.

3. **Invest in yourself**. The number one thing you can do to achieve your goals and dreams in life, is to invest in yourself. You invest in yourself by doing three things on a regular basis.

Number one is reading books every single day. You must read books on success, business, and money management if you're going to succeed. Number two is listening to audio cd's every single day. You must listen to audio cd's on success, business, and money management if you're going to succeed. Number three is going to training events every single week. The Network Marketing company you're in should have training events every single week that you can plug into and learn from successful people. If they don't, that is a sure sign to realize that is not the right company to be with. You must invest in training. This includes local, regional, and international events. If your company has a training event scheduled, you need to be there. The more training events you attend, the more money you will earn.

4. **Be 100% coachable**. If you're with the right company and have the right mentor, then be 100% coachable to everything they teach you. If your company is successful, and if your mentor is successful, then what they're doing is obviously working. Do what they do and you'll have what they have. This is guaranteed.

These are the only four tips you need to follow to become successful in Network Marketing. I always tell people, you know the right thing to do, now you just have to do it. If you're ready for the right company, the right mentor, and ready to invest in training and be 100% coachable, contact me and I'll personally help you achieve all your goals and dreams in life. I look forward to working with you very soon. God bless you!
www.ChangeYourLifeOvernight.com

Now that you've read this book, would you mind doing me a HUGE favor please? Would you be kind enough to write me a five-star customer review for this book on Amazon? By giving this book a good review it will help me as an author and help more people be able to find the book on Amazon. Your words do have power. If you would be kind enough to write me a good customer review for this book, I would greatly appreciate it. I love hearing from people who have read my books. Please feel free to contact me any time. I wish you the very best of success in every area of your life!
www.ChangeYourLifeOvernight.com

If you enjoyed reading this book, here's more books by the author:

-Sell Your First Book

-Vision Board Success

-Faith Produces Miracles

-My Inspiring True-Life Story

-Money Meditation Manifestation

-Why You're Fat & Sick And How To Fix It

-How To Lose Weight With Intermittent Fasting

-Success! The Secret To Becoming Happy, Healthy, And Wealthy

-How To Make Money As An Author Selling Your Books On Amazon

All books can be purchased from:
www.amazon.com/author/fitchristophermitchell

www.ingramcontent.com/pod-product-compliance
Lightning Source LLC
Chambersburg PA
CBHW050235230526
45470CB00005B/1958